P9-DBL-303

Media Center
Lake Shore Elementary School
Pasadena, MD

910 GRE
2162281365
Greve, Meg
LAKE SHORE ELEMENTARY SCH

North, South, East, and West

Meg Greve

Media Center
Lake Shore Elementary School
Pasadena, MD

ROURKE PUBLISHING
Vero Beach, Florida 32964

© 2010 Rourke Publishing LLC

All rights reserved. No part of this book may be reproduced or utilized in any form or by any means, electronic or mechanical including photocopying, recording, or by any information storage and retrieval system without permission in writing from the publisher.

www.rourkepublishing.com

PHOTO CREDITS: © Alexander Kosev: Title Page, 22; © cyrop: 3; © Ian Cumberland: 3, 6, 10, 11 © Jan Rysavy: 4, 6, 8, 10, 12, 14, 16, 18, 20, 22, 23; © gisele: 5; © sweetym: 5, 9, 13, 17, 21; © digitalskillet: 7; © clu: 9; © Wolfgang Schoenfeld: 11; © jabejon: 13; © Kim Gunkel: 15; © David Hernandez: 17; © Olga Solovei: 19; © Jani Bryson: 21; © slobo: 23; © Derris Lanier: 23

Edited by Jeanne Sturm

Cover design by Nicola Stratford bppublishing.com
Interior design by Tara Raymo

Library of Congress Cataloging-in-Publication Data

Greve, Meg.
North, south, east, and west / Meg Greve.
p. cm. -- (Little world geography)
Includes bibliographical references and index.
ISBN 978-1-60694-418-9 (hard cover)
ISBN 978-1-60694-534-6 (soft cover)
1. Cardinal points--Juvenile literature. 2. Orientation--Juvenile literature.
I. Title.
G108.5.C3G74 2010
910--dc22

2009006020

Printed in the USA

CG/CG

www.rourkepublishing.com - rourke@rourkepublishing.com
Post Office Box 643328 Vero Beach, Florida 32964

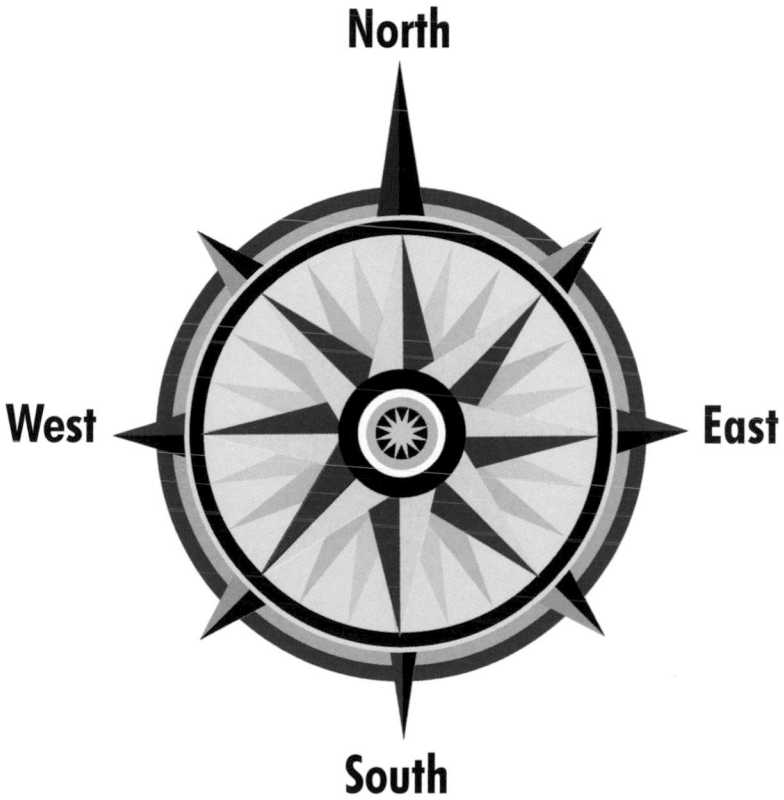

North, south, east, or west, a **compass rose** helps you know which way to go.

Where is north?

North?
Hmmmm...

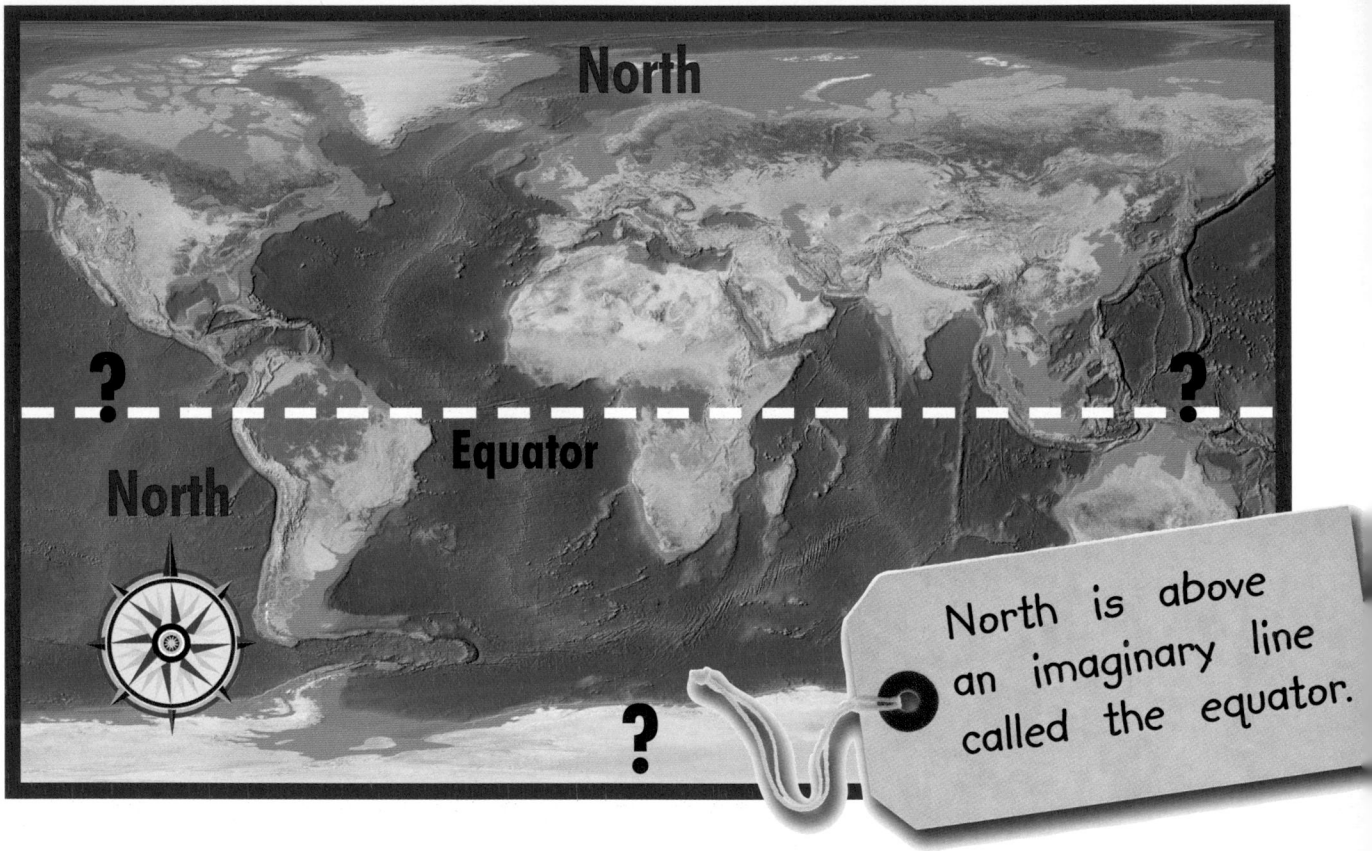

At the **top** of the **map.**

Brrrr!

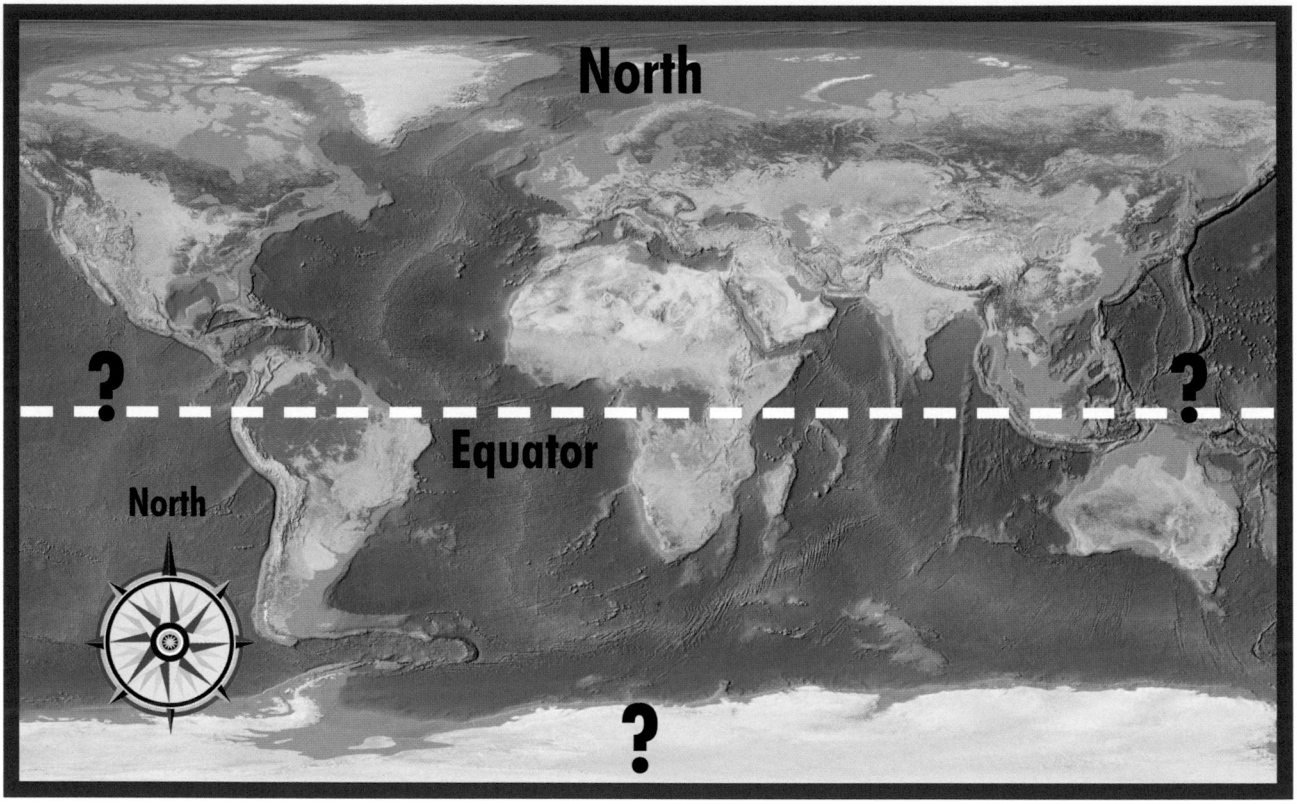

Where is south?

South?
Hmmmm...

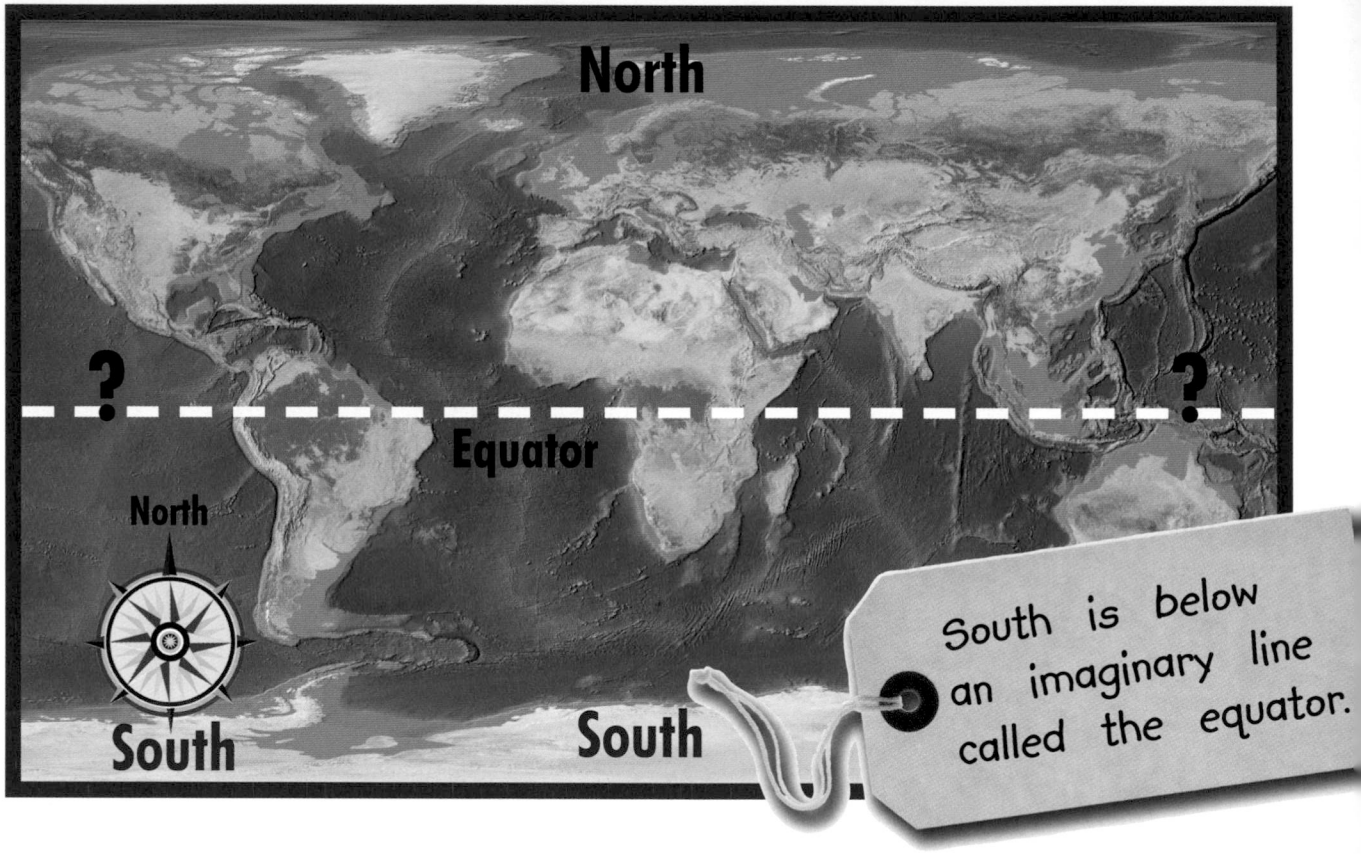

At the **bottom** of the map.

Brrrr!

The North and South Poles are very cold places where very few things live.

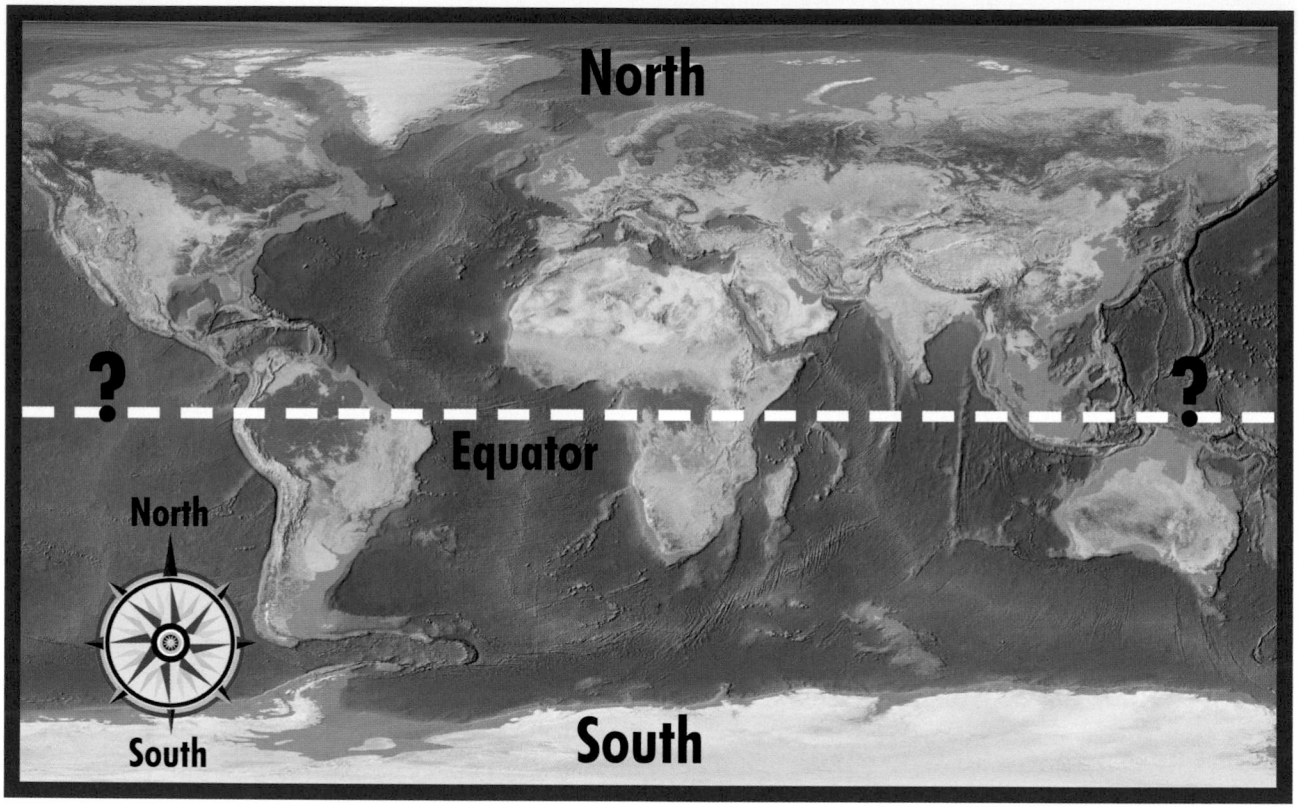

Where is east?

East?
Hmmmm...

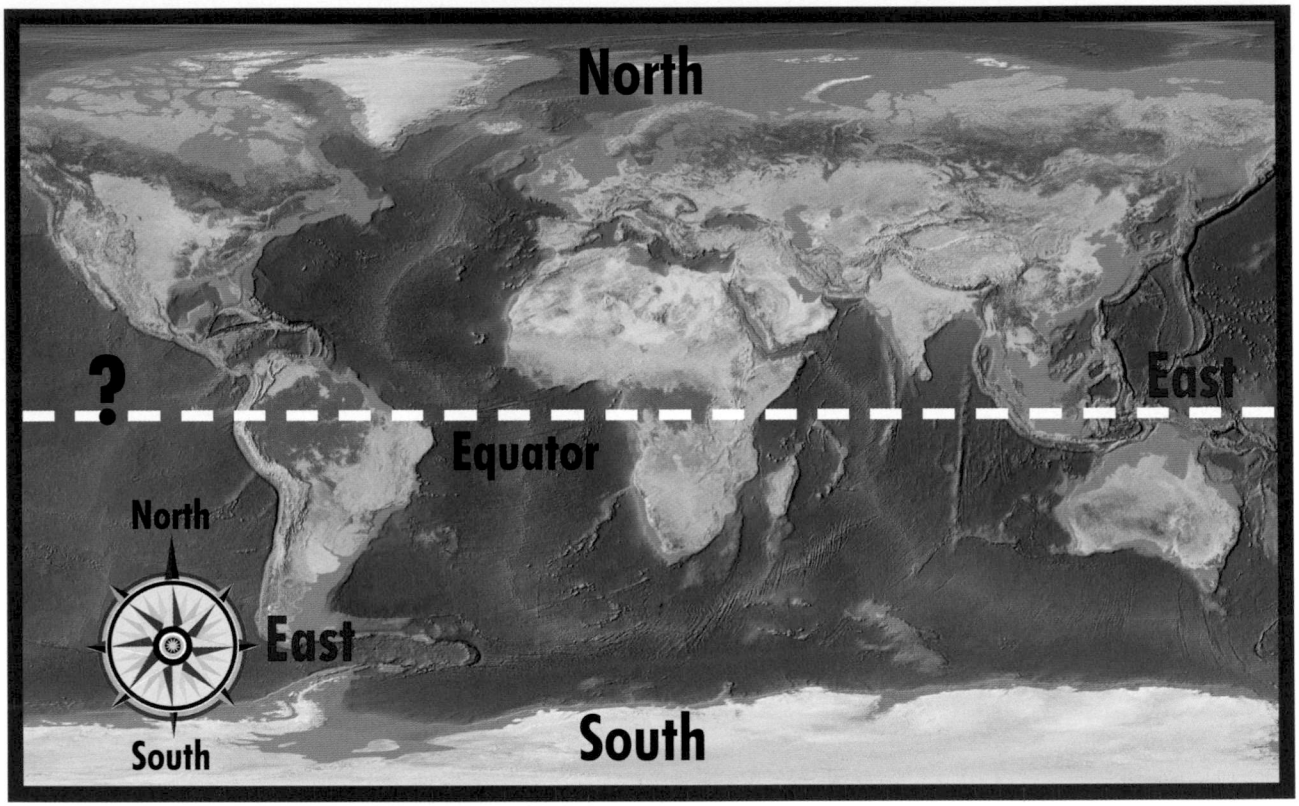

On the right of the map,
where the **Sun** rises.
Good morning!

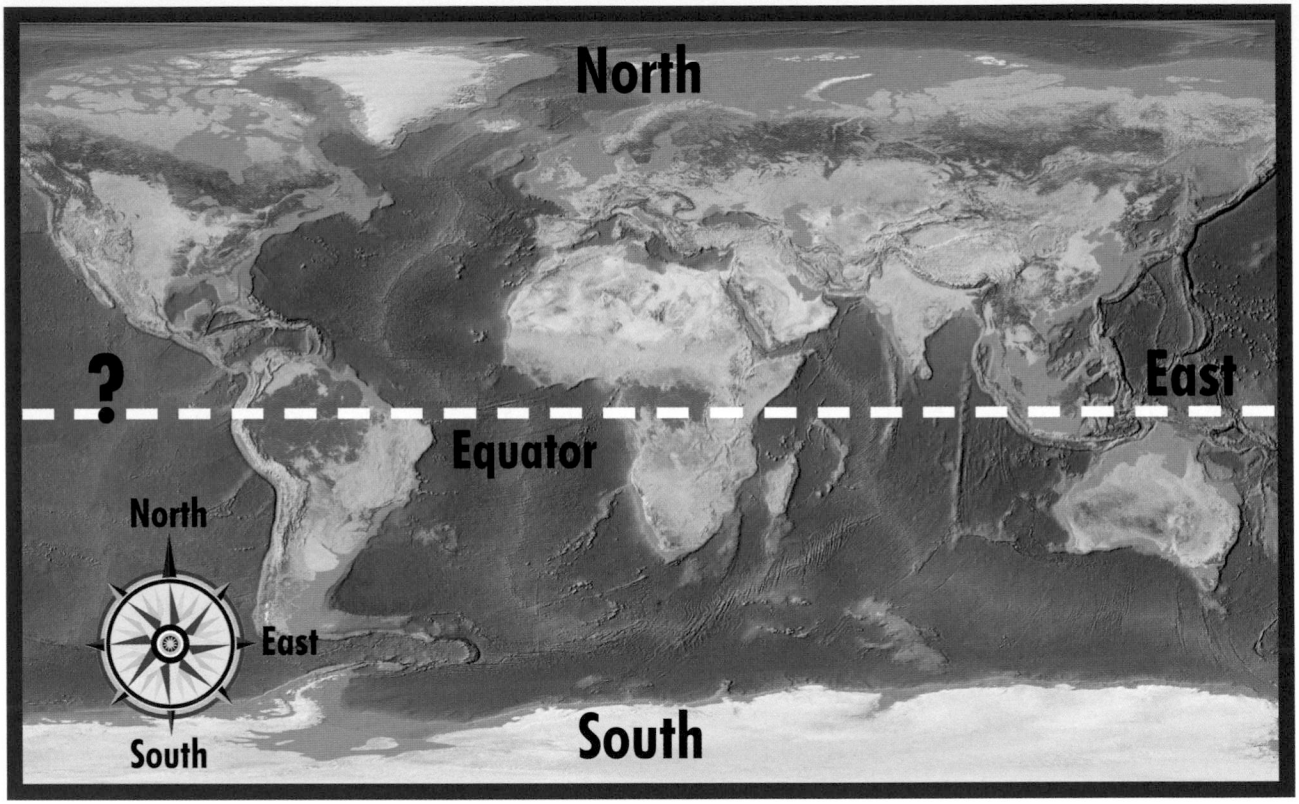

Where is west?

West?
Hmmmm...

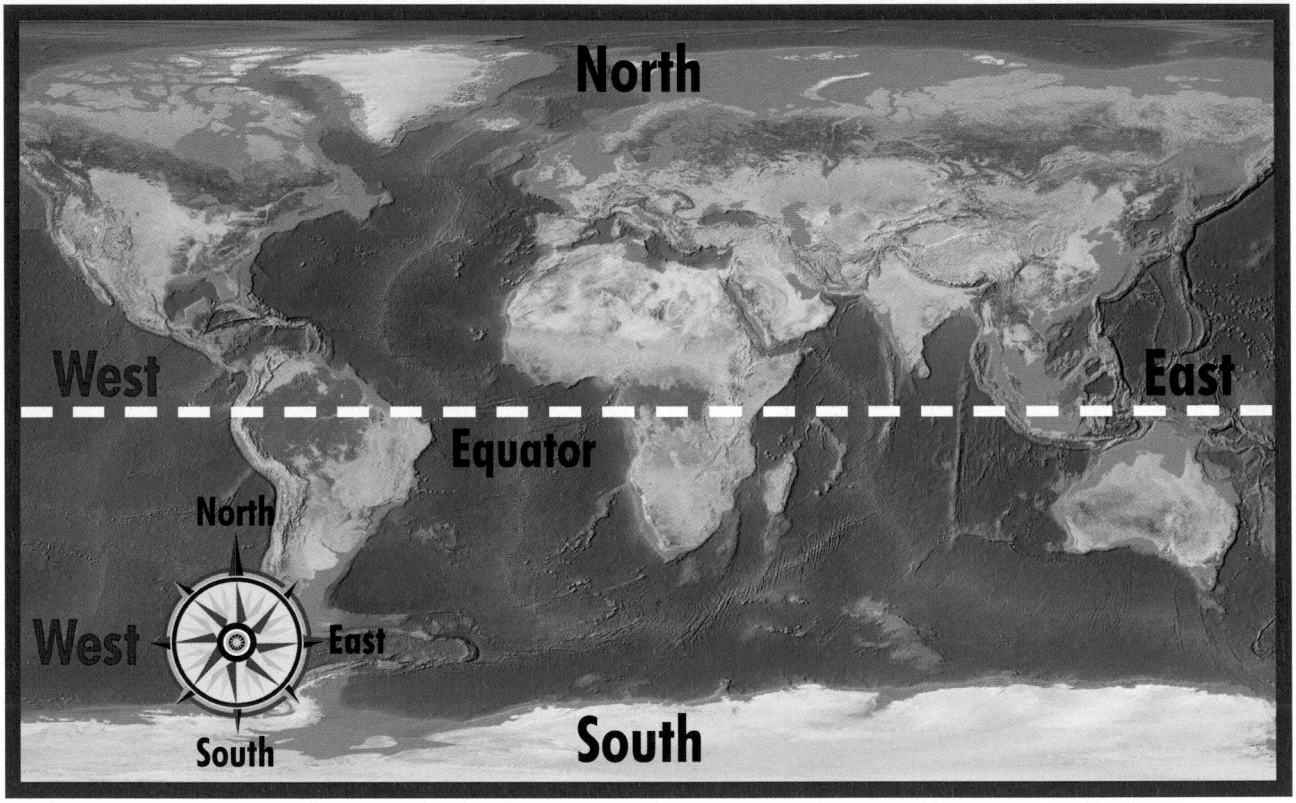

On the left of the map, where the Sun sets.

Good night!

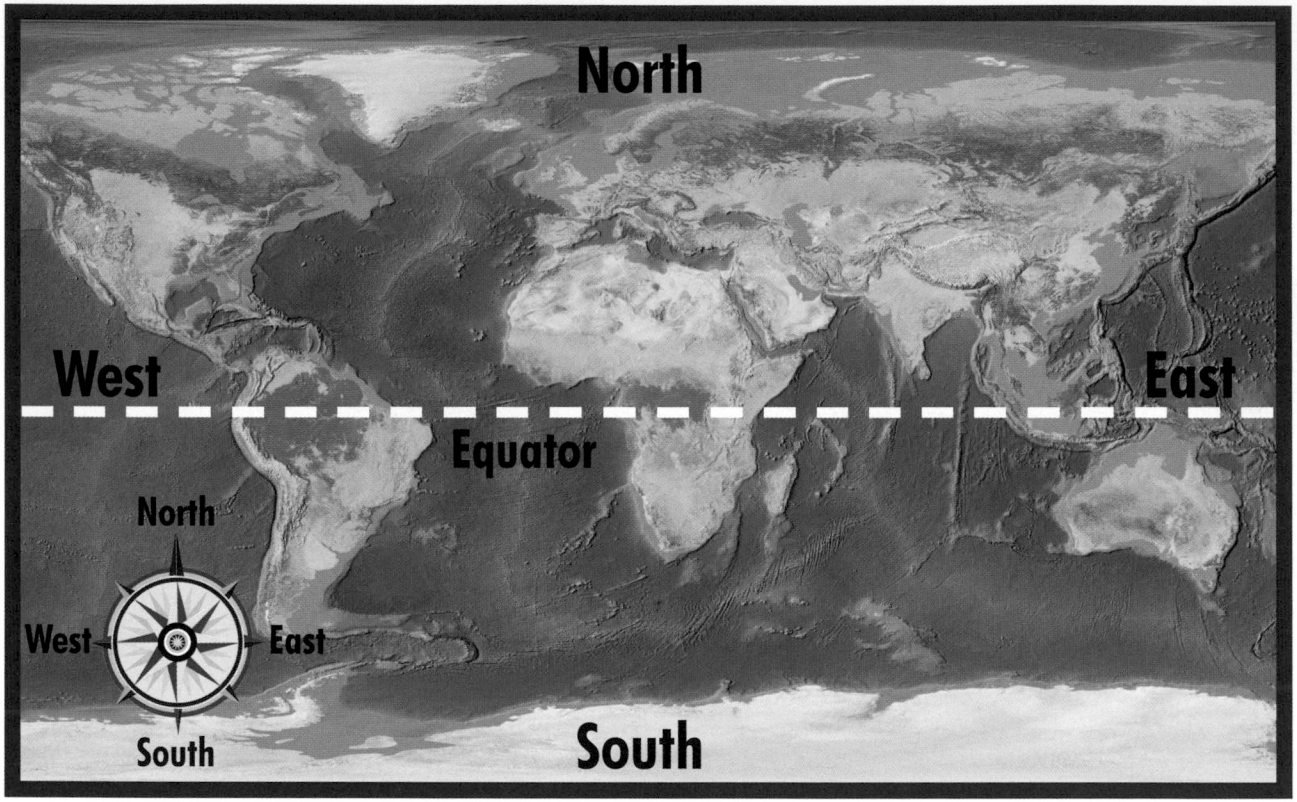

North, south, east, west, which **direction** do you like best?

north
south
east
west

GLOSSARY

bottom (BOT-uhm): The bottom is the lowest part of something. On a map, the bottom is south.

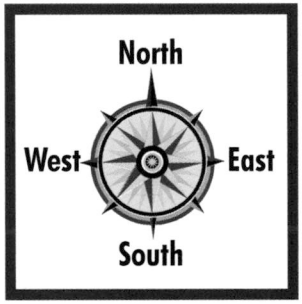

compass rose (KUHM-puhss ROZE): A compass rose is found on a map. It is a circle with points that shows directions, such as north, south, east, and west.

direction (duh-REK-shuhn): A direction is the way that someone or something is going. North, south, east, and west are special directions we use when reading a map or telling the location of something.

map (MAP): A flat drawing of an area. There are maps of streets, towns, cities, the world, and much more. Maps contain symbols and colors, which all stand for something larger.

Sun (SUHN): The Sun is the only star in our solar system. All of the planets revolve around the Sun. The Sun provides light and heat for the Earth.

top (TOP): The top is the highest part of something. On a map, the top is north. Always keep north at the top when you read a map.

Index

direction 20
east 3, 12, 20
map 6, 10, 14, 18
north 3, 4, 6, 20
south 3, 8, 10, 20
Sun 14, 18
west 3, 16, 20

Websites to Visit

www.maps4kids.com
www.fedstats.gov/kids/mapstats/
kids.nationalgeographic.com/

About the Author

Meg Greve lives in Chicago with her husband, daughter, and son. She loves to study maps, but still gets lost sometimes!